THE
ASTROLOGY
DICTIONARY

.... ✦ ....

COSMIC KNOWLEDGE
FROM A TO Z

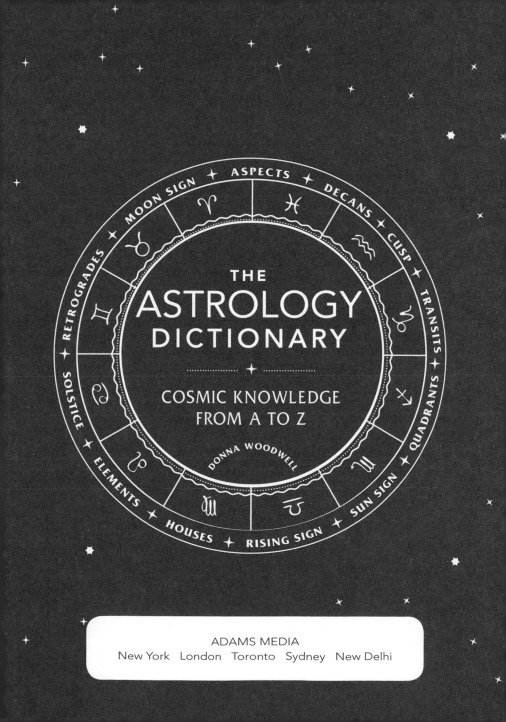

THE
ASTROLOGY
DICTIONARY

COSMIC KNOWLEDGE
FROM A TO Z

DONNA WOODWELL

MOON SIGN · ASPECTS · DECANS · CUSP · TRANSITS · QUADRANTS · SUN SIGN · RISING SIGN · HOUSES · ELEMENTS · SOLSTICE · RETROGRADES

ADAMS MEDIA
New York London Toronto Sydney New Delhi

Adams Media
An Imprint of Simon & Schuster, Inc.
57 Littlefield Street
Avon, Massachusetts 02322

This Adams Media hardcover edition August 2020

ADAMS MEDIA and colophon are trademarks of Simon & Schuster.

For information about special discounts for bulk purchases, please contact Simon & Schuster Special Sales at 1-866-506-1949 or business@simonandschuster.com.

The Simon & Schuster Speakers Bureau can bring authors to your live event. For more information or to book an event contact the Simon & Schuster Speakers Bureau at 1-866-248-3049 or visit our website at www.simonspeakers.com.

Interior design by Michelle Kelly
Images © 123RF/Pavlo Kovernik, Roman Sotola, painterr

Manufactured in the United States of America

4 2021

ISBN 978-1-5072-1533-3

FOR MY ASTROLOGY STUDENTS

Introduction

How will Mercury retrograde affect your relationships? What is an astrological age and what does this mean for the world around us? How can a midheaven help you recognize and achieve your full potential?

Astrology is a rich and varied tradition spanning centuries. The ancient Indian, Chinese, and Mayan civilizations, as well as other ancient cultures, developed elaborate systems of reading significance into the movements of the planets, stars, and other celestial objects. These systems have been handed down the centuries, preserving their wisdom for today's turbulent age. Unsurprisingly for such an ancient discipline, astrology has many dimensions, which is why this dictionary was created: to help you understand this fascinating subject.

The Astrology Dictionary gives you the most important and influential terms necessary to understand twenty-first-century astrology. These are the words you'll see most often in astrology discussions and analyses of horoscopes, whether online, in books, or in person. These words, commonly used in astrology, will help you to better understand your chart. That, in turn, will give you more insight into the world around you. You'll find these terms and phrases organized in alphabetical order. Sometimes, to define one term, it's necessary to refer to another term; when that's the case, we've put the word or phrase in boldface. If you're unsure what that boldfaced word means, look it up under its own entry and you'll find more information about it.

If you're just beginning to explore the world of astrology and want to find definitions for terms you're coming across, you'll find that information here. Or, if you're already studying astrology and want to elevate your practice, these entries and their definitions will help inform your reading and give you a deeper understanding of your charts and horoscope. No matter where you are on your astrological path, this book will help you learn not just what these important astrology terms and phrases mean, but also how these concepts have been used to improve lives in both practical and spiritual ways. And what they've done for others, they will do for you too. So start at the beginning of the alphabet and work your way through the book, or just begin with a term that interests you and move forward. Either way, understanding awaits.

Definitions

accidental dignity, *noun*

An accidental dignity occurs when a **planet** gains strength based on its location in a **chart** relative to astrological factors other than **Zodiac signs**. For example, a planet **conjunct** an angle, or located in an **angular house**, or is heliacally rising, possesses accidental dignity.

✦

Age of Aquarius, *noun*

Popular culture and New Age thought look forward to the Age of Aquarius as a time of greater consciousness and social harmony. Other sources have linked the Aquarian Age to the current period of scientific evolution, to technological advance, to democracy, and to the desire for self-determination. There is much discussion about when the Age of Aquarius will begin—or, indeed, if it already has begun. **Astrologers** have suggested a range of **astrological age** start dates for it—including, for example, 1500 c.e., more than five hundred years ago, and the year 2500 c.e.

✦

Age of Pisces, *noun*

The Age of Pisces is associated with a rise in interest in personal religious and transcendental experience, greater exploration of life after death, the rise of compassion-centered religions, as well as the growth of large religious-centered organizations and governing structures. **Astrologers** have given a range of dates for the ending of the Age of Pisces; these include 1500 C.E. (in which case it ended more than five hundred years ago) and 2500 C.E.

───────── ✦ ─────────

air sign, *noun*

Zodiacal signs are each associated with one of the four Greek **elements**: air, fire, water, and earth; the Greeks believed these four elements made up the physical universe. The air element creates a desire to be more social, intellectual, and communicative. **Libra**, **Aquarius**, and **Gemini** are the **Zodiac**'s three air signs.

───────── ✦ ─────────

Aldebaran, *noun*

Aldebaran marks the right eye of the Bull in the **constellation Taurus**. This **fixed star** lends an earthy, lusty, shrewd-in-business, or materialistic tone to nearby **planets** or **chart angles**. Aldebaran is one of the four **royal stars**, along with **Regulus**, **Antares**, and **Fomalhaut**. In **astrological magic**, Aldebaran is known as the Watcher of the East and is associated with the archangel Michael. Due to **precession**, Aldebaran currently sits at 9 **degrees** 47 minutes of the **Tropical Zodiac** sign **Gemini**.

angular house, *noun*

Planets located in angular houses are prominent players in a **chart**; they are often expressed outwardly in your personality, relationships, or vocation. Their meanings are derived from their association with **chart angles**. Angular houses include the **First**, **Fourth**, **Seventh**, and **Tenth houses**.

＋

Antares, *noun*

Antares marks the heart of the Scorpion in the **constellation Scorpio**. This **fixed star** lends an intense, driven, passionate, successful, or obsessive quality to nearby **planets** or **chart angles**. Antares is one of the four **royal stars**, along with **Aldebaran**, **Regulus**, and **Fomalhaut**. In **astrological magic**, Antares is known as the Watcher of the West and is associated with the archangel Uriel. Due to **precession**, Antares currently sits at 9 **degrees** 47 minutes of the **Tropical Zodiac** sign **Sagittarius**.

＋

Aquarius, *noun*

The Aquarius **constellation** is the Water Bearer, a human carrying a large barrel of water.

This **fixed Saturn**-ruled **air sign** doesn't mind being different; an Aquarian is strong enough not to compromise principles just to get along. But Aquarians are also smart enough to know they've got to harmonize with the crowd to create effective change in the world.

This sign is intellectual, abstract, and detached, not emotional or passionate. It's not hard to get an Aquarian to debate you, but getting one to be emotionally present and embodied may be a different matter.

Modern astrology sometimes associates Aquarius, as the eleventh **Zodiac sign**, with the **Eleventh House** via the **natural house** overlay. Several decades after the discovery of **Uranus**, **astrologers** began associating it with Aquarius.

⋯⋯⋯ ✦ ⋯⋯⋯

Aries, *noun*

Aries is the **cardinal Mars**-ruled **fire sign**. Its **constellation** is the Ram. When there's no path, it takes all of this sign's strength and courage to break out in a new direction.

A single-minded vision, however, has a few drawbacks. An Aries doesn't have much use for compromise. Take-charge Aries want to surround themselves with folks who can take the heat. Though Aries are quick to anger, they are also equally quick to forget and move on. Of all the signs, Aries is the least concerned with relationships. Romance, sexual heat, sure. Competition to win their lover's heart, no problem. But once they've conquered, they need new challenges in order to feel fulfilled.

Modern **astrologers** sometimes associate Aries, as the first **Zodiac sign**, with the **First House** via the **natural house** overlay.

Aries point, *noun*

The Aries point is the first **degree** of the **Tropical Zodiac**. It's also the location of the **Sun** at the Northern **Hemisphere**'s Spring **Equinox**. When astrology **charts** were invented by the Hellenistic Greeks, the Aries point was situated in the **constellation** Aries, but due to **precession** it now sits in the constellation **Pisces**. The Aries point is also one of the four points on the **world axis**.

...... + ...

ascendant, *noun*

The ascendant marks the place where the **Sun**, **Moon**, and **planets** appear to rise above the horizon in the East. The ascendant represents you and your physical form—your body, your life, and your personal style. The **Zodiac sign** in which the ascendant sits is called the **rising sign**.

Hellenistic astrology named the ascendant the *horoskopos*, from which we derive the word *horoscope*. In most **house systems**, the ascendant is associated with the **First House**. Since the location of the ascendant determines all other **houses**, ancient **astrologers** considered it the most powerful point in an astrology **chart**.

The point opposite the ascendant is called the **descendant**; both are **chart angles**.

aspect, *noun*

An aspect describes the quality of the relationship between two **planets** in an astrological **chart**. The word *aspect* derives from the Latin word *aspicere*, which means "to see" or "to behold"; planets in aspect can see each other.

There are three types of aspects. Aspects by **Zodiac sign** are formed by planets in signs that share a **polarity**, **triplicity**, or **sign mode**. Aspects by **degree** measure the angular distance between two planets along the **ecliptic** in degrees of celestial longitude. *In mundo* aspects are those based on the visual relationship between planets in the sky.

Aspects are also divided into major (or Ptolemaic) aspects and minor aspects. Major aspects include the **conjunction**, **sextile**, **square**, **trine**, and **opposition**.

The strength of an aspect's influence is determined by the **orb** of the aspect; the more precise the aspect, the stronger its impact.

✦

aspect pattern, *noun*

When three or more **aspects** occur together to form a larger structure, it is called an aspect pattern. Examples include T-**squares**, grand **trines**, and grand **sextiles**. **Charts** with aspect patterns are rare and may signify a powerful or intense gathering of energy.

aspectarian, *noun*

An aspectarian is a chronological list of all astrological **aspects** occuring during a particular time range. Aspectarians are often published in calendar form, including wall calendars, weekly desk calendars, pocket calendars, or plug-ins for calendar apps. They are used in **astrological forecasting** to predict the cosmic vibe of the day.

······ + ······

asteroid, *noun*

Asteroids are the collection of millions of small bodies orbiting in the inner solar system; most are found in the asteroid belt between **Mars** and **Jupiter**. Four of the largest asteroids— **Ceres** (now considered a dwarf planet by astronomers), **Vesta**, **Juno**, and **Pallas**—have been widely used by **astrologers** since their discovery in the 1800s. Today, computer-aided **astrology** has enabled some astrologers to add thousands of additional asteroids to astrology **charts**. Asteroid meanings are often derived from the mythology of their namesake.

······ + ······

astrologer, *noun*

Someone who studies or practices **astrology** is called an astrologer. The term *astrologist* is considered incorrect or offensive by many astrologers.

astrological age, *noun*

An astrological age is a period, approximately 2,150 years, during which historical and cultural events take on the flavor of the **Zodiac sign** the **Sun** occupies at the Spring **Equinox**. There are twelve astrological ages during the 26,000-year cycle known as **precession**. Most **astrologers** say we are currently moving from the **Age of Pisces** into the **Age of Aquarius**, though there is little agreement on specific dates for the transition.

+

astrological forecasting, *noun*

Astrological forecasting techniques compare the current, changing sky to the natal **chart** in order to make predictions about upcoming life events. When forecasting, **astrologers** often analyze supplementary charts, such as **transits**, **progressions**, **solar arcs**, and **planet returns**, to provide clues as to when opportunities or challenges may arise and when they might end.

+

astrological magic, *noun*

Astrological magic uses auspicious planetary alignments or **planetary hours**, in conjunction with plants, stones, and other objects with a sympathetic resonance to **planets**, to encourage desired mental states or terrestrial events. Astrological magic often makes use of **electional astrology charts**, talismans, mantras, and rituals to connect heavenly and earthly energies.

astrology, *noun*

Astrology refers to the study of the subtle or metaphysical correspondence between the movements of heavenly bodies and human or earthly affairs. The earliest astrological imagery dates back thirty-five thousand years; indigenous cultures from around the world show numerous examples of shamanic star lore and divination. By combining the mathematics, **astronomy**, philosophy, and mythology of earlier cultures, Hellenistic **astrologers** developed the recognizable forerunners of the astrology **chart** still in use today. **Hellenistic astrology** inspired the further development of **Western astrology, Indian astrology,** and **Chinese astrology.**

⋯⋯⋯⋯ ✦ ⋯⋯⋯⋯

Astronomical Zodiac, *noun*

The International Astronomical Union (IAU) officially recognizes thirteen zodiacal **constellations** of unequal widths, which cross the **ecliptic**. These include the twelve familiar **Zodiac** constellations, as well as **Ophiuchus**, the Snake Charmer. The confusion between the Astronomical Zodiac and the twelve **Zodiac signs** used by **astrologers** has led to the occasional news story about Zodiac signs changing.

astronomy, *noun*

Astronomy is the study of the physical nature of the **fixed stars**, **planets**, **asteroids**, **centaurs**, and other celestial objects using scientific techniques and measurements. Astronomy and **astrology** were considered part of the same practice until the seventeenth century during the period of the Scientific Revolution, at which time astronomers divorced themselves from their astrological spouse.

······················ ✦ ······················

benefic, *adjective*

Benefic derives from the Latin word *beneficius*, meaning "kindness," "charity," or "good fortune." The benefic **planets Venus** and **Jupiter** are associated with events that bring ease, pleasure, or abundance.

······················ ✦ ······················

Black Moon Lilith, *noun*

In the early part of the twentieth century, theosophical **astrologers** linked the **Moon**'s apogee point with dark goddess energy, calling it the Black Moon Lilith. Following the Lilith mythology, the point evokes shadows, feminine power, wildness, untamed sexual energy, and self-empowerment. The Moon's perigee point has been called **Priapus**; together, Priapus and Lilith represent the **lunar apsides**.

cadent house, *noun*

Cadent means "falling away" or "declining." Traveling via its daily motion through the **houses**, the **Sun** declines in power once it moves past a **chart angle** into a cadent house. Consequently, **planets** situated in cadent houses are said to require more effort to exert themselves in the world. The cadent houses are the **Third, Sixth, Ninth**, and **Twelfth houses**.

························ ✦ ························

Cancer, *noun*

Cancer leads with its emotions, as befits a **cardinal water sign** ruled by the **Moon**. It will place protecting its family, team members, or tribe above other concerns. Cancer uses its natural empathy and nurturing skills to care for those in its flock.

But Cancer, whose **constellation** is the Crab, has learned from hard experience it needs its protective shell and razor-sharp pincers. Anger a Cancerian or threaten their safety and you'll feel the hard, sharp side of both. Cancerians instinctively know where your soft spots are. They are attached to the past, so their memories are long. Friends and family of a Cancerian are blessed, so long as the Crab feels safe. If not, batten down for an emotive assault or some masterful moody manipulation.

In **modern astrology**, Cancer—as the fourth **Zodiac sign**—is associated with the **Fourth House** via the **natural house overlay**.

Capricorn, *noun*

Capricorn's **constellation** is the Sea Goat, a goat's head and torso with a fish's tail. This **cardinal Saturn**-ruled **earth sign** is at its best when hard work, pragmatism, and self-discipline win out over emotionalism and projected fears. Of course, for every upside, there's a down. For Capricorns, there's a tendency to look at their feet as they climb. But if their self-discipline is balanced with an appreciation of beauty, pleasure, humor, and empathy, Capricorns can have it all.

The key to being in a relationship with a Capricorn is simple: You're always expected to be your best. So, if you're looking for coddling, a Capricorn isn't the right fit for you. But if you're looking to be your best self, they will challenge you to be accountable.

In **modern astrology**, Capricorn—as the tenth **Zodiac sign**—is associated with the **Tenth House** via the **natural house** overlay.

$$\cdots\cdots\cdots \quad + \quad \cdots\cdots\cdots$$

cardinal sign, *noun*

Cardinal signs mark the beginning of each of the four **seasons**. They are active, dynamic, enterprising, or crisis-oriented. The cardinal signs—**Aries**, **Cancer**, **Libra**, and **Capricorn**—are also known as the **world axis**.

centaur, *noun*

Centaurs are likely **trans-Neptunian objects** (TNOs) that have migrated into orbits between the **planets** of **Jupiter** and **Neptune**. They exhibit qualities of both **asteroids** and comets, and are consequently named for the human-horse hybrid of Greek mythology. **Chiron** was the first officially recognized centaur. **Astrologers** are just starting to investigate the significance of other centaurs, including Chariklo, Nessus, Pholus, and Asbolus.

⋯⋯ ✦ ⋯⋯

Ceres, *noun*

The **asteroid** Ceres, named for the Roman goddess of grain who lost her daughter to the king of the underworld, represents themes of motherhood, nurturing, the harvest, food and eating, nourishing, and mother-daughter bonds. The largest asteroid in the asteroid belt, Ceres is now considered a dwarf **planet** by astronomers, the same status granted to **Pluto**, Eris, and other minor planets.

⋯⋯ ✦ ⋯⋯

Chaldean order, *noun*

The Chaldean order lists the visible **planets** from the slowest moving to the fastest, i.e., **Saturn**, **Jupiter**, **Mars**, the **Sun**, **Venus**, **Mercury**, and the **Moon**. This order determines the **planetary hours**, as well as **decan rulerships** in some systems.

chart, *noun*

An **astrology** chart is a stylized map of the sky, depicting the position of the **Sun, Moon**, and **planets** as viewed from a particular time and place on the Earth. To the creators of astrology, a chart represented the divine or spiritual intentions of a given moment in time, or the cosmic material in which an incarnating soul is clothed.

Though charts—sometimes called birth charts, natal charts, or chart wheels—may vary for different forms of astrology, they typically include planets, **Zodiac signs**, **houses**, and **aspects**.

A date, place, and time of a birth or other event are required to accurately cast a chart. Before the modern age, personal **natal astrology** charts were accessible only by the very wealthy.

⁜ ✦ ⁜

chart angle, *noun*

A chart's four angles are the **ascendant** and **descendant**, and **MC (*medium coeli*)** and **IC (*imum coeli*)**. The origin of the term *angle* derives from the fact that the earliest **astrology charts** were square, not round; these points are associated with the **angular houses** in the square chart—the **First, Fourth, Seventh**, and **Tenth houses**. To the ancient **astrologers**, these four points also marked the location at which the soul entered the material plane; **planets** located near these points were considered the strongest in a chart.

Chinese astrology, *noun*

Chinese astrology blends Chinese lunar **astrology**, **five-element** theory, philosophy, and mathematics with a few elements imported from **Hellenistic astrology** to create a unique system used in Chinese medicine, feng shui, and the *I Ching*, also known as the *Book of Changes*. The Chinese **Zodiac**, however, differs from Hellenistic **Zodiac signs**; its symbols are the Rat, Ox, Tiger, Rabbit, Dragon, Snake, Horse, Goat, Monkey, Rooster, Dog, and Pig.

✦

Chiron, *noun*

Chiron is a minor **planet** found between the orbits of **Saturn** and **Uranus**, the first of a class of objects now called **centaurs**. Ancient Greek myths about Chiron the centaur creature suggest its astrological meaning, including healing, teaching, and maverick tendencies.

✦

conjunction, *noun*

Planets form an **aspect** known as a conjunction when they are very near each other in the sky. Depending on the planets involved, a conjunction may suggest an easy or a problematic relationship—a beautiful healthy friendship or a willingness to drive over a cliff together. Conjunctions between planets symbolize beginnings, new cycles, initiations, concentration, intensity, strength, empowerment, prominence, focus, and unification. The strength of a conjunction depends on the **orb** between the planets involved and is usually 8 **degrees** or less.

constellation, *noun*

A constellation is a grouping of **fixed stars**, usually associated with mythological creatures or stories. Diverse cultures have identified unique constellations. The constellations identified in the Babylonian-Greek-Arabic star lore tradition are those used by **Western astrology** as well as the International Astronomical Union (IAU).

························ ✦ ························

decan, *noun*

A decan is a 10-**degree** division of a **Zodiac sign**; there are three decans per sign, and thirty-six decans along the **ecliptic**. Originally part of the Egyptian calendar, each decan was associated with one or more **fixed stars** and Egyptian deities. Incorporating the Egyptian calendar with astrology **charts**, **Hellenistic astrology** associated each decan with a ruling **planet** and considered it a minor form of **essential dignity**. Decans, also known as "faces" because of their association with images of deities, have also been blended into **astrological magic** practices.

························ ✦ ························

degree, *noun*

A degree is the unit of measurement used to describe the location of **planets** along the **ecliptic** in celestial longitude. The 360-degree ecliptic is broken into twelve 30-degree segments, called **Zodiac signs**. Degrees may be further divided by minutes and seconds—1 degree equals 60 minutes, and 1 minute equals 60 seconds.

descendant, *noun*

The decendant marks the place where the **Sun, Moon,** and **planets** disappear below the horizon in the West. The descendant represents significant others in your life—your partner or spouse, or rivals, competitors, and enemies. In most **house systems,** the descendant is associated with the **Seventh House.** The point opposite the descendant is called the **ascendant**; both are **chart angles.**

························· ✦ ·························

detriment, *noun*

A **planet** is in detriment when located in a **Zodiac sign** opposite its **rulership.** Planets in detriment may find it challenging to express their essential natures, requiring conscious effort or creative reinterpretations to function well in the world. Though planets in detriment may struggle, detriment is still considered an **essential dignity.**

························· ✦ ·························

earth sign, *noun*

Zodiacal signs are each associated with one of the four Greek **elements:** air, fire, water, and earth; the Greeks believed these four elements made up the physical universe. The earth element keeps our feet on the ground, and so earth signs seek to express themselves in physical, practical ways. **Capricorn, Taurus,** and **Virgo** are the earth signs.

eclipse, *noun*

Eclipses are considered extremely potent **New Moons** or **Full Moons** and may herald significant changes in your life if they connect with your natal **chart**. An eclipse occurs when the **Earth**, **Moon**, and **Sun** are directly aligned along the nodal axis, also called the **lunar nodes**. Solar eclipses occur when the New Moon passes directly between the Earth and the Sun, covering all or part of the Sun's disk. A lunar eclipse occurs when the Earth sits between the Sun and Moon, casting a shadow on the Full Moon. Eclipse season happens twice each year, and usually contains one solar and one lunar eclipse.

······················ ✦ ······················

ecliptic, *noun*

The ecliptic traces the **Sun**'s apparent path across the background of **fixed stars** throughout Earth's one-year orbit. Other **planets** follow this path, since most travel around the Sun along the same flat disk as the Earth. However, other planets take more or less time to complete their circle depending on their distance from the Sun.

Constellations that cross the ecliptic are known as the **Astronomical Zodiac**, from which the **Zodiac signs** take their names. The intersection of the ecliptic path with local compass points forms the basis of the framework for casting **astrology charts**. The word *ecliptic* comes from the word *eclipse*, since eclipses occur at the places where the **Moon**'s orbit crosses the ecliptic.

Eighth House, *noun*

As it enters the Eighth House, the **Sun** prepares to set for the day. Consequently, the Eighth House represents going into the shadows. It's a place of taboos, shame, and criminals. It's the **house** of death, since the dead travel to the underworld.

It's also considered one of the money houses. As the house of death, it governs inheritance. The Eighth House is a **succedent house**, so it contains what supports the **Seventh House**. That includes jointly held funds, money involving spouses or partnerships, and money that is owed to others.

Planets located in the Eighth House don't make a major **aspect** with the **ascendant** and therefore require more effort to make their expression conscious.

The Eighth House sits opposite the **Second House**. **Modern astrology,** via the **natural houses** overlay, links the Eighth House with **Scorpio**, **Mars**, **Pluto**, or all of them. Some modern **astrologers** also associate the Eighth House with sex.

···················· ✦ ····················

electional astrology, *noun*

Using astrological techniques to find auspicious dates for important events is called electional astrology. Examples include good dates for exchanging wedding vows, putting a house on the market, filing business incorporation papers, or starting a vacation. Electional astrology is closely related to **astrological magic.**

element, *noun*

In ancient times, elements referred to the basic constituents of matter from which all things are made.

Greek philosopher Empedocles suggested four elements—fire, earth, air, and water—as essential components of the natural world. **Hellenistic astrology** incorporated these elements as the names of the **Zodiac sign triplicities**.

Chinese astrology and philosophy features five elements—water, metal, fire, wood, and earth. The visible **planets** were named for these elements—**Mercury** as "water star," **Venus** as "metal star," **Mars** as "fire star," **Jupiter** as "wood star," and **Saturn** as "earth star."

✦

Eleventh House, *noun*

The Eleventh House contains all the things that uplift us and support our work in the universe. In a perfect world, this includes our friends, trade associations, support groups, spiritual communities, charities, and philanthropic connections. It also contains our spirit guides, guardian angels, or conscience, as well as our hopes and wishes for our future success. Its original name was the House of the Good Spirit, and it is the **planetary joy** of **Jupiter**.

The Eleventh House is a **succedent house**. As the **house** that supports the **Tenth House**, the Eleventh House holds your salary, as well as any professional counselors, mentors, or advisors for the professional work that you do.

The Eleventh House sits opposite the **Fifth House**, the planetary joy of **Venus**.

Modern astrology, via the **natural house** overlay, associates the Eleventh House with **Aquarius**, **Saturn**, **Uranus**, or all of them.

ephemeris, *noun*

An ephemeris is a book or digital table that lists daily **planet positions** by **Zodiac degree**. It is an essential tool for calculating astrology **charts** and for **astrological forecasting**.

.... ✛ ....

equal houses, *noun*

One of the idealized **house systems**, equal houses use twelve 30-**degree** divisions of the **ecliptic** to mark **house cusps**. The house cusps usually repeat the degree of the **ascendant** through other **Zodiac signs**, though other important points have also been used. Equal houses are often employed in **astrological forecasting**, since entrance into a new **house** also forms an **aspect** with a **chart angle** or other important point.

.... ✛ ....

equinox, *noun*

A term meaning "equal night," the equinox marks the beginning of spring or fall **seasons**, a time of year when the day and night are of equal length. In the **Tropical Zodiac**, equinoxes occur when the **Sun** enters **Aries** or **Libra**. These signs form part of the **world axis**. In the Northern **Hemisphere**, the Spring Equinox falls at 0 **degrees** Aries, and the Fall Equinox at 0 degrees Libra; in the Southern Hemisphere, this is reversed.

essential dignity, *noun*

A **planet** has essential dignity when situated in a **Zodiac sign** that supports or enhances its archetypal nature. There are several forms of essential dignity—**rulership** and **detriment**, **exaltation** and **fall**, **triplicity**, bounds, and **decans**.

⁘ ✦ ⁘

evolutionary astrology, *noun*

Evolutionary astrology is a branch of **modern astrology** that seeks to understand the development of the soul through lifetimes. Evolutionary **astrologers** often combine elements from transpersonal psychology, theosophy, Indian philosophy, and channeling in their interpretations. They tend to emphasize the **planets Uranus**, **Neptune**, and **Pluto**, as well as the **lunar nodes**.

⁘ ✦ ⁘

exaltation, *noun*

Though exaltation is one of the oldest concepts in **Hellenistic astrology**, the origin of the exaltations of **planets** by **Zodiac sign** and by **degree** remains uncertain. Planets located in their sign of exaltation are raised up by the sign, able to express their best selves. Each **cardinal sign** serves as an exaltation for one of the planets—the **Sun** is exalted in **Aries**, **Jupiter** in **Cancer**, **Saturn** in **Libra**, and **Mars** in **Capricorn**. Other planets are arranged with a similar logic—the **Moon** is exalted in **Taurus**, **Venus** in **Pisces**, and **Mercury** in **Virgo**. A planet is in **fall** when located in the sign opposite its exaltation.

experiential astrology, *noun*

Experiential astrology is a catchall category that includes the use of shamanism, astrodrama (using a chart as an outline for a kind of improv), guided visualization, or hypnosis to work directly with astrological symbolism and archetypes as tools for healing or self-discovery. Experiential astrology leads naturally to the practice of **astrological magic** and ritual.

+

fall, *noun*

A **planet** is in fall when located in the **Zodiac sign** opposite its **exaltation.** Though planets in fall may struggle to express their best selves, with conscious effort they may learn to function well in the world. While planets in fall may face challenges, fall is still considered an **essential dignity.**

+

Fifth House, *noun*

The Fifth House contains all acts of pleasure—romance, vacations, playtime, gambling, and anything else fun. Its original name was the House of Good Fortune, and it is the **planetary joy** of **Venus.**

The Fifth House is a **succedent house.** As the **house** that supports the **Fourth House,** the Fifth House contains children, as well as estate managers.

The Fifth House sits opposite the **Eleventh House,** the planetary joy of **Jupiter.**

Via the **natural house** overlay, **modern astrology** associates the Fifth House with the **Zodiac sign Leo**, the **Sun**, or both. Its modern key words also include *creativity* and *sex*.

······· ✦ ·······

fire sign, *noun*

Zodiacal signs are each associated with one of the four Greek **elements**: air, fire, water, and earth; the Greeks believed these four elements made up the physical universe. The fire element creates energy, passion, and heat. Consequently, fire signs are exciting, enthusiastic, and direct. **Aries**, **Leo**, and **Sagittarius** are fire signs.

······· ✦ ·······

First House, *noun*

The First House contains *you*—your body, your appearance, and your style. It also represents how you "dawn" on the world—not surprising since the First House sits where the **Sun** rises in the East.

The First House straddles the divide between day and night. It's the **planetary joy** of **Mercury**, suggesting that Mercury's reason, communication, and mindfulness are the ideal ways to approach life.

The **ascendant** is associated with the First House, which makes it one of the **angular houses**. It sits opposite the **Seventh House**.

Via the **natural house** overlay, **modern astrology** associates the First House with **Aries, Mars**, or both.

fixed sign, *noun*

The fixed **sign mode** falls in the middle of **seasons**; its energy feels stabilizing, nurturing, and value-oriented. The fixed signs are **Taurus, Leo, Scorpio**, and **Aquarius**.

The fixed signs are portrayed in biblical and occult literature as creatures symbolizing the four directions or four "corners" of the world; their symbols are the Bull (Taurus), the Lion (Leo), the Eagle (Scorpio), and the Human or Water Bearer (Aquarius).

✦

fixed star, *noun*

The term *fixed stars* refers to the background of stars across which **planets**—the "wandering stars"—move in the night sky. In the days of **Hellenistic astrology, astrologers** believed the fixed stars were affixed to a celestial sphere that encircled the Earth beyond the planets. Patterns in the fixed stars form **constellations**, including those after which the **Zodiac signs** are named. The four bright fixed stars associated with the **fixed signs** are called **royal stars**.

✦

Fomalhaut, *noun*

Fomalhaut sits at the foot of the Water Bearer (the **constellation Aquarius**) in the modern constellation Piscis Austrinus. This **fixed star** lends an ethereal, romantic, or intoxicated flavor to nearby **planets** or **chart angles**. Fomalhaut is one of the four **royal stars**, along with **Aldebaran, Regulus**, and **Antares**.

In **astrological magic**, Fomalhaut is known as the Watcher of the South and is associated with the archangel Gabriel. Due to **precession**, Fomalhaut currently sits at 3 **degrees** 52 minutes of the **Tropical Zodiac** sign **Pisces**.

──────── ✦ ────────

Fourth House, *noun*

The Fourth House sits at the bottom of the **chart**. When the **Sun** is in the Fourth House, it's the middle of the night and the Sun is hidden from view by the limb of the Earth. To the ancients, it was traveling through the underworld.

Consequently, the Fourth House represents what grounds you—your roots. This includes your biological roots—your lineage, heritage, and ancestors—as well as family traditions, lands, and estate. It also represents your psychological roots, such as complexes from childhood or even the collective unconscious.

The Fourth House is one of the **angular houses**. The **IC** (*imum coeli*) marks the cusp of the Fourth House in **quadrant house systems**. It sits opposite the **Tenth House**.

Via the **natural house** overlay, **modern astrology** associates the Fourth House with **Cancer**, the **Moon**, or both.

Full Moon, *noun*

A Full Moon occurs when the **Sun** and **Moon** are on opposite sides of the Earth and the Moon's whole disk is illuminated. During a Full Moon, the Sun and Moon form an **opposition**. Full Moons mark the middle of the **lunation cycle**. They symbolize culmination and fulfillment; they are regarded as emotionally potent moments.

············ ✦ ············

Gemini, *noun*

Smartphones and social media may have been invented by Gemini, the **Mercury**-ruled **air sign** whose **constellation** is the Twins. The active minds of Geminis crave constant stimulation and a steady diet of new sensations. Curiosity drives their hunger. Only plugging into pure perception can provide them with any lasting satisfaction—if they are willing to empty their minds long enough to experience it. Geminis know full well that "fear of missing out" is a temptation hard to resist.

Life with a Gemini is certainly never boring. A social butterfly by nature, they'll be the witty conversationalist at any party. But if you're looking for exclusivity, this sign's **mutable** nature and taste for variety may be more than you'd bargained for.

Modern astrology associates Gemini, as the third **Zodiac sign**, with the **Third House** via the **natural house** overlay.

Hellenistic astrology, *noun*

Hellenistic-age **astrologers** invented what's now known as horoscopic **astrology** approximately twenty-two hundred years ago. This ancient melting pot of Greek, Egyptian, and Babylonian cultures combined indigenous **fixed star** lore with innovations in mapmaking and philosophy to create the first astrology **charts**, ones that can still be read by today's astrologers. **Electional astrology** and **horary astrology** were the earliest forms of astrology. The first astrologers also cast and interpreted personal **horoscopes**, though only the very wealthy had recorded birth times with which to calculate.

·················· ✦ ··················

hemisphere, *noun*

The major **chart angles** divide the **chart** into hemispheres, one half of a circle.

The Southern Hemisphere lies above the **ascendant** and **descendant** axis. **Planets** in the Southern Hemisphere are more likely to want to express themselves in the external, objective world. The Northern Hemisphere sits beneath the ascendant and descendant axis. Planets in the Northern Hemisphere may be more comfortable acting in the inner, subjective realms.

The Eastern Hemisphere sits on the left side of the **MC (*medium coeli*)** and **IC (*imum coeli*)** axis. Planets in the Eastern Hemisphere may be individualistic and self-motivating. The Western Hemisphere sits on the right side of the MC and IC axis. Planets in the Western Hemisphere may be more reactive or motivated by relationships.

Each hemisphere may be further divided into two **quadrants**.

horary astrology, *noun*

Like tarot cards and other forms of divination, **astrology** can be used to find answers to very specific questions, such as "Where are my lost keys?" or "Will I get this job?" or "Where's the cat?" Horary astrology is the branch of astrology that analyzes the **chart** of the moment a question is asked in order to discover clues to the answer.

.... ✦ ....

horoscope, *noun*

In **Hellenistic astrology**, a horoscope meant an **astrology chart**. However, in modern times a horoscope has become synonymous with **Sun sign** horoscopes. These simplified examples of **astrological forecasting** are written for the position of the **Sun** in relationship to each **Zodiac sign** and are therefore accessible to those who know only their date of birth and not necessarily the time or place of birth.

.... ✦ ....

house, *noun*

The astrological houses are twelve divisions of an **astrology chart**, each relating to a different area of life or human concern, such as health, family, relationships, and vocation. In **traditional astrology**, the meanings are generated by the **planetary joys**, **planetary sect**, and the relationship of the houses to the **chart angles**. **Modern astrology** also uses a **natural house** overlay to link **Zodiac signs** to houses. The location of **house cusps** is determined by the choice of **house system**.

house cusp, *noun*

The house cusp is the starting point of an astrological **house**, usually marked by a line and the **degree** at which the house begins.

.... ✦ ....

house modes, *noun*

There are three house modes—**angular, succedent,** and **cadent.** Modes indicate the position of a **house** in relationship to the **chart angles.** Modes are also known as quadruplicities.

.... ✦ ....

house ruler, *noun*

The house ruler is the **planet** that rules the **Zodiac sign** on a **house cusp.** It takes responsibility for the area of life described by the house. A house ruler is sometimes called a house lord, or lord of the house.

house system, *noun*

There are numerous ways to divide up a three-dimensional sky into **houses**. As a result, **astrologers** have created at least twenty-four different house systems.

Idealized houses are based on equal divisions of the **ecliptic** (**whole sign** and **equal houses**). **Quadrant** houses are based on dividing the sky by space (Porphyry system, Regiomontanus system, etc.) or time (**Placidus** system, Koch system, etc.).

House systems are a point of contention among astrologers, since the choice of system can move **planets** from one house into another, changing the **chart** interpretation. Some astrologers assert different house systems are useful for exploring different branches of **astrology**. Others suggest different systems are useful for casting charts for different physical locations. In the past, most astrologers used whatever house system their teacher used. This practice has become more complex in the age of the Internet since astrologers using different systems are in more regular contact with one another.

.... ✦ ....

IC (*imum coeli*), *noun*

IC is short for *imum coeli*, Latin for "bottom of the sky" or "deepest sky." The IC is hidden by the Earth's horizon; to ancient **astrologers**, it represented the underworld.

In a natal **chart**, the IC is related to ancestry, lineage, genetics, heritage, and psychological roots. **Planets** and **Zodiac signs** associated with the IC are often reflected by your family, parents, or psychological health.

In some **house systems**, the IC marks the start of the **Fourth House**. The point opposite the IC in a natal chart is the **MC** (*medium coeli*), and together they form a major chart axis.

inconjunct, *noun*

An inconjunct **aspect**, also called a quincunx, occurs when two **planets** are separated by 150 **degrees**. Inconjuncts suggest adjustments are required for the planets involved to work harmoniously. The strength of an inconjunct depends on the **orb** between the planets involved and is usually 2–3 degrees or less.

✦

Indian astrology, *noun*

Hellenistic astrology traveled east and mixed with the rich existing **astronomy** and **astrology** of India. Together, they created what's now known as Indian astrology, Vedic astrology, or *Jyotish*, the "science of light." Unlike practitioners of **Western astrology**, most Indian **astrologers** use the **Sidereal Zodiac**. A **Lunar Zodiac** known as the **Nakshatras** is another powerful influence. Indian astrology also emphasizes religious rituals and other remedies to balance planetary energies, similar to the techniques of **astrological magic.**

✦

Juno, *noun*

The **asteroid** Juno, named for the wife of **Jupiter** and queen of the gods, represents themes involving marriage, queenship, conception, childbirth, finance, jealousy, commitment, and betrayal.

Jupiter, *noun*

Jupiter spends approximately one year in each **Zodiac sign** during his orbit around the **Sun**. To align with Jupiter means to live in right-relationship with the divine, to have integrity, to act justly, and to bestow mercy. Jupiter governs revelations, wise counsel, and advice.

Jupiter, known as the greater **benefic**, inspires generosity and gratitude. He signifies advocating for others—sharing support, encouragement, wealth, and abundance. He encourages us to have faith and optimism, to be open to possibilities.

Negatively applied, Jupiter leads to feeling entitled, self-righteous, opportunistic, pompous, overextended, or greedy.

Jupiter rules the **Zodiac signs Sagittarius** and **Pisces**. His **planetary joy** is the **Eleventh House**. Thursday is Jupiter's day of the week. In **astrological magic**, colors aligned with Jupiter in **Indian astrology** are saffron yellow and orange; in **Western astrology**, his colors are royal blue and purple. His alchemical metal is tin.

Via the **natural house** overlay, **modern astrology** associates Jupiter with the **Ninth House**.

.... ✦ ....

Leo, *noun*

This **Sun**-ruled **fire sign** may feel the urge to put on a good show. With their natural flair for the dramatic, and impeccable sense of style, Leos are often at the center of the party.

However, sometimes this **fixed sign** needs to take itself less seriously; playtime helps the Lion, Leo's **constellation**, recharge its batteries.

If you're in a relationship with a Leo, showing how much you value their gifts is a way to their heart. If there's something you need, pretend you're asking the king (or queen) for a favor. They are usually generous souls if they don't feel as if they've been given an ultimatum.

Modern astrology associates Leo, as the fifth **Zodiac sign**, with the **Fifth House** via the **natural house** overlay.

.... ✦ ....

Libra, *noun*

Beauty, harmony, and love are Libra's forte. So naturally this **cardinal Venus**-ruled **air sign** advocates for good manners, tolerance, and respect for all voices, as long as others are willing to do the same. Unfortunately, there's a downside—Libras can find it hard to make any choice at all.

Even when Libras know what they want, they won't tell you—this way, they avoid conflict. You'll have to guess, and then face judgment from the Scales, Libra's **constellation**, for guessing wrong. Libras thrive on a steady diet of agreement, loving praise, and tokens of affection. If you must disagree with one, remember that patience, civility, and a heaping spoonful of sugar help cure most relationship ills—eventually.

Modern astrology associates Libra, as the seventh **Zodiac sign,** with the **Seventh House** via the **natural house** overlay.

locational astrology, *noun*

Locational astrology seeks to discover auspicious places for a person to pursue various activities, such as establishing a comfortable home, finding romance, achieving career satisfaction, or making money. This relatively new kind of **astrology** has been made possible by the introduction of computers to help with calculating the relationships between a **chart** and the Earth's surface. The most popular form of locational astrology is called Astro*Carto*Graphy.

······· ✦ ·······

lunar apsides, *noun*

Apsides refer to the closest point to and the farthest point from a central body in an orbit. For the **Moon**, the apsides are called *perigee*, meaning "close to the Earth," and *apogee*, meaning "far from the Earth."

As the Moon nears its perigee, it appears larger than usual and moves faster; the fast Moon is associated with quick, perceptive thinking. The **New Moon** or **Full Moon** at perigee is also called a **supermoon**.

When the Moon nears its apogee, it appears smaller and moves slower. This slow Moon signifies patient, deliberate consideration. The New Moon or Full Moon at apogee is called a micromoon.

Modern astrology sometimes calls the Moon's apogee **Black Moon Lilith**, and the perigee **Priapus**.

Like the **lunar nodes**, the apsides represent points in space, rather than physical bodies.

lunar mansions, *noun*

In **Western astrology**, the twenty-eight **Lunar Zodiac** signs are called lunar mansions. The term *mansion* likely derives from the Arabic *manzil*, the nightly resting places for a desert-crossing caravan. Medieval Arabic **astrologers** aligned the lunar mansions with the **Tropical Zodiac**, asserting that all things should rightly fall under the auspices of the **Sun**. Used primarily in medieval and Renaissance **astrological magic**, lunar mansions fell out of widespread use in the time of **modern astrology**. One remaining trace are the so-called critical **degrees**, the twenty-eight 12-degree, 51-minute divisions of the Tropical Zodiac marking the start of lunar mansions.

...............✦...............

lunar nodes, *noun*

The lunar nodes mark the two points where the **Moon**'s orbit intersects with the **ecliptic**, the **Sun**'s apparent path across the sky. The node at which the Moon rises north of the ecliptic is called the ascending or **north node**; the opposite node where the Moon crosses south of the ecliptic is called the descending or **south node**. As crossing points of the Sun and Moon, the lunar nodes also mark where solar and lunar **eclipses** occur.

In **relationship astrology**, the lunar nodes are indicators of intense connections between **charts**. In **evolutionary astrology**, the nodes are frequently used as indicators for soul growth and evolution.

Like the **lunar apsides**, the nodes represent points in space, rather than physical bodies.

Lunar Zodiac, *noun*

Likely the first **Zodiac**, the Lunar Zodiac features twenty-seven or twenty-eight signs based on the **Moon**'s monthly orbit, invented for plotting the position of the Moon over time. Since the Moon takes approximately twenty-seven-and-a-third days to orbit the Earth, it spends one night in each Lunar **Zodiac sign**. The Lunar Zodiac may be aligned with the **Sidereal Zodiac** (as are the **Nakshatras** in **Indian astrology**) or the **Tropical Zodiac** (as are the **lunar mansions** in **Western astrology**).

These lunar signs are usually named for themes related to **fixed stars** contained within them. **Astrologers** assign governing **planets** to each Lunar Zodiac sign. The most popular use of the Lunar Zodiac in Western astrology is in **astrological magic**.

✦

lunation cycle, *noun*

The lunation cycle describes the phases of the **Moon** through its monthly orbit of the Earth. The cycle begins with the **New Moon**, then increases in light through the Waxing Crescent, First Quarter, and Waxing Gibbous phases, to culminate as a **Full Moon**. The Moon then decreases in light, becoming Waning Gibbous, Last Quarter, and Waning Crescent before returning to its New Moon phase. The cycle symbolizes the birth, growth, fulfillment, decay, death, and rebirth of natural events. Rituals tied to the lunation cycle are popular in **astrological magic**.

malefic, *adjective*

Malefic derives from the Latin word *maleficus*, meaning "misfortune" or "difficulty." The malefic **planets Mars** and **Saturn** may signify difficult events, or those that require hard work or effort to resolve well.

＋

Mars, *noun*

His ruddy glow links Mars with blood and war. Mars strengthens, fortifies, protects, defends, and stands firm.

Unlike the inner **planets Mercury** and **Venus**, Mars can appear anywhere in the night sky along the **ecliptic**. His vibe helps us to break away, to pioneer, to compete. Mars will inspire you to sacrifice for your principles.

Known as the lesser **malefic**, fiery Mars signifies things that stimulate, burn, anger, or explode. An unskilled or negatively expressed Mars can turn violent, reckless, cruel, enraged, and destructive.

Mars rules the **Zodiac signs Aries** and **Scorpio**. His **planetary joy** is the **Sixth House**. Tuesday is Mars's day of the week. In **astrological magic**, Mars's color is red. His alchemical metal is iron. The adjective associated with Mars is *martial*.

Via the **natural house** overlay, **modern astrology** associates Mars with the **First** and **Eighth houses**.

MC (*medium coeli*), *noun*

MC is short for *medium coeli*, which is Latin for "middle of the sky." The MC is more commonly called the **midheaven**.

.... ✦ ....

medical astrology, *noun*

Medical astrology is used to answer questions about the cause of an illness, the period it might last, the best herbs or medicines to use for a cure, and the timing of when to administer that cure. The subject was once taught at universities; doctors used the techniques of medical astrology until well into the 1800s. Medical astrology is often used in conjunction with herbalism; this combination is similar to traditional Chinese or Ayurvedic medicine.

.... ✦ ....

Mercury, *noun*

Mercury circles the **Sun** in just eighty-eight days. He's the fastest-moving **planet** across our sky, with the most frequent **retrogrades**.

Mercury switches between ideas and opportunities quickly, acquiring knowledge, inventing, assimilating new ideas, and analyzing. He's also quick to joke.

Mercury's the master of all forms of communication. He oversees business and other transactions—he negotiates, exchanges, barters, and advertises. He is also involved with divination, **astrology**, magic, and ritual.

Mercury has a dark side too: lying, cheating, wheeling and dealing, engaging in con artistry, and stealing.

Mercury rules the **Zodiac signs Gemini** and **Virgo**. His **planetary joy** is the **First House**. Wednesday is Mercury's day of the week. In **astrological magic**, Mercury's colors are varied: yellows, oranges, browns, spring green, and mottled colors. His alchemical metal is quicksilver (mercury). The adjective associated with Mercury is *mercurial*.

Via the **natural house** overlay, **modern astrology** associates Mercury with the **Third** and **Sixth houses**.

⋯⋯⋯⋯ ✦ ⋯⋯⋯⋯

Mercury retrograde, *noun*

When Mercury is **retrograde**, **astrologers** predict communication mishaps, travel delays, and computer malfunctions. While all **planets** turn retrograde, Mercury retrogrades three times each year, more than any other.

⋯⋯⋯⋯ ✦ ⋯⋯⋯⋯

midheaven, *noun*

As the most elevated point on the **ecliptic** at the moment a **chart** is cast, the midheaven symbolizes your highest potential. In a natal chart, the midheaven is related to your calling or purpose in the world. **Planets** and **Zodiac signs** linked with the midheaven are often reflected in your career, your status in the world, or your reputation.

The point opposite the midheaven in a natal chart is the **IC (*imum coeli*)**; both mark **chart angles**.

In **quadrant house systems**, the midheaven marks the start of the **Tenth House**. It is also called the **MC (*medium coeli*)**.

.... ✦ ....

midlife transits, *noun*

Midlife transits are a series of three transiting **aspects** involving **Uranus**, **Neptune**, and **Saturn**, usually encountered by someone between the ages of thirty-nine and forty-four, which mark a period of heightened change or psychological and spiritual growth. Popularly known as a midlife crisis, midlife transits are one of several pivotal celestial alignments that lead many to seek astrological advice for the first time.

.... ✦ ....

modern astrology, *noun*

Due to the changes brought about by the Scientific Revolution, **Western astrology** nearly died out. But the discovery of new **planets** and **asteroids**, as well as spiritualist and mystical movements, rekindled interest during the nineteenth century. Since some of the theoretical underpinnings of **astrology** had been lost, modern astrology reinvented itself with new ideas drawn from theosophy, psychology, and science. Branches of modern astrology multiplied in the twentieth century, to include **psychological astrology, evolutionary astrology, experiential astrology**, harmonic astrology, and numerous others. Most focus on **natal astrology, astrological forecasting**, and, to a lesser degree, **mundane astrology**.

Modern astrology stands apart from **traditional astrology** through its inclusion of new planets such as **Uranus, Neptune, Pluto,** and others, as well as its use of the **natural house** overlay to assign **house** meanings.

$$\cdots\cdots\cdots \text{\Large +} \cdots\cdots\cdots$$

Moon, *noun*

Mistress of the night, the Moon's gravity stabilizes our climate and allows life to evolve and thrive. So the Moon symbolizes things that nurture and protect. Since she sheds no light of her own, the Moon's associated with gathering and receiving. Memory and nostalgia are functions of the Moon.

While her form changes, the pattern of change remains predictable. Consequently, the Moon represents the capacity to handle change, as well as actions that are familiar.

The unskilled uses of the Moon's energies include codependency, intoxication, emotional irrationality, the tendency to become stuck in habits or routines, or the feeling of being victimized by fate and addictions.

The Moon rules the **Zodiac sign Cancer.** Her **planetary joy** is the **Third House.** Monday is the Moon's day of the week. In **astrological magic,** the Moon's colors are cool, ranging from white to gray, blue, and black. Her alchemical metal is silver. The adjective associated with the Moon is *lunatic.*

Via the **natural house** overlay, **modern astrology** associates the Moon with the **Fourth House.**

Moon sign, *noun*

As the **Zodiac sign** in which the **Moon** is located, your Moon sign indicates how you feel safe and comfortable, what your emotional outlook is, how you form habits, and how your subconscious mind works. **Modern astrology** considers the Moon sign, **Sun sign**, and **rising sign** as the three factors that, taken together, best summarize overall personality and character.

Moon signs may also refer to the signs found in the **Lunar Zodiac**, such as the **Nakshatras** or **lunar mansions**.

------ ✦ ------

mundane astrology, *noun*

Mundane astrology seeks to answer questions related to politics, business, society, and natural events, such as "Who will win the election?" or "Which stocks will do well this year?" Mundane **astrologers** search for answers by using **charts** of the founding of countries, cities, or corporations, or the birth of leaders, political candidates, or others in the news. Mundane astrology is used to plan the best time for investing (financial astrology), for planting and harvesting crops (agricultural astrology), and for predicting the weather (astrometeorology) and earthquakes (geological astrology).

mutable sign, *noun*

The mutable **sign mode** marks the **season**'s end; mutable signs are changeable, adaptable, transformative, negotiatory, or fickle. **Gemini**, **Virgo**, **Sagittarius**, and **Pisces** are the mutable signs.

+

Nakshatra, *noun*

Nakshatras, used primarily in **Indian astrology**, are a twenty-seven-sign **Lunar Zodiac** that predates the twelve solar **Zodiac signs** imported from **Hellenistic astrology**. Nakshatras are used both in **natal astrology** and in **astrological forecasting**. These 13-**degree** 20-minute sections of the **ecliptic** are described in Indian astro-mythology as the twenty-seven wives of the **Moon** god Chandra. The Moon's Nakshatra sign is as important as the **Sun sign** in **modern astrology**; it was once traditional to name babies in honor of this **Moon sign**.

+

natal astrology, *noun*

If you've ever sought out an **astrologer** for advice about your life, you're already familiar with what's called natal astrology. This is primarily used for answering basic questions such as "Why am I here?" "What's my vocation?" or "How can I become more happy and content?" Astrologers use an astrology **chart** cast for the moment of birth to understand character, vocational strengths, spiritual growth, and more about your essential nature.

natural houses, *noun*

Natural houses is a term used to describe a **house system** overlay that associates the **First House** with the first **Zodiac sign, Aries**; the **Second House** with the second sign, **Taurus**; and so on. A variant of the natural houses, known as the "twelve-letter alphabet," has been used primarily in **modern astrology** since the 1970s to explain the meanings of **houses**.

+

Neptune, *noun*

Like the other "invisible" outer planets **Uranus** and **Pluto**, Neptune is associated with processes that move us beyond the physical. Dreamlike and elusive, Neptune's a **planet** of "no boundaries," or even "nonbeing." His action idealizes, spiritualizes, and fantasizes. Wherever Neptune is, we might be called to sacrifice, to relinquish, to let go, to surrender, or to forsake.

He seeks dissolution, intoxication, escape, or anesthesia— anything to get away from the pain and weight of the three-dimensional world. It's easy to fall under the spell of too much Neptune. An unskillful or negative experience of Neptune includes a loss of identity, delusions, deception, lies, weakened focus, lack of clarity, lack of boundaries, or a desire to escape existence itself.

Modern **astrologers** associate Neptune with the **Zodiac sign Pisces**. Via the **natural house** overlay, Neptune and Pisces are linked to the **Twelfth House**.

New Moon, *noun*

A New Moon occurs when the **Sun** and **Moon** meet on the same side of the sky, and the Moon is invisible to observers on Earth. During a New Moon, the Sun and Moon form a **conjunction**. New Moons begin the **lunation cycle**, and therefore symbolize beginnings. In **astrological magic**, they are regarded as auspicious times to set intentions for the coming month.

＋

Ninth House, *noun*

In **Hellenistic astrology**, the Ninth House was called the House of the Sun God, the **planetary joy** of the **Sun**. As the cosmic lawgiver, the Sun's **house** held all things that promoted exploration of the divine order—philosophy, established religion, the law, higher education, and the like. The Greek's Sun god, Apollo, oversaw the Oracle of Delphi, and so prophecies, dreams, divination, and **astrology** also found their place in the Ninth House. In ancient times, these practices often required a pilgrimage, so long-distance travel joined the other Ninth House activities.

The Ninth House is one of the **cadent houses**. Its opposite—the **Third House**—is known as the House of the **Moon**.

Via the **natural house** overlay, **modern astrology** associates the Ninth House with **Sagittarius**, **Jupiter**, or both.

north node (of the Moon), *noun*

The north **lunar node**, also called the ascending node, Dragon's Head, or Rahu, represents yearnings, compulsions, and new cycles. In karmic and **evolutionary astrology**, the north node's **Zodiac sign** and **house** location indicate the direction toward which the soul is growing.

············ ✦ ············

Ophiuchus, *noun*

Called the **Zodiac**'s thirteenth **constellation**, Ophiuchus—the Snake Charmer—was added to the International Astronomical Union (IAU) official collection of **ecliptic-crossing** constellations of the **Astronomical Zodiac** in 1930. The **fixed stars** within this constellation are associated with healing, doctors, and snakes. Most **astrologers** do not consider Ophiuchus to be a **Zodiac sign**, since by definition, there can never be more than twelve signs.

············ ✦ ············

opposition, *noun*

Planets separated by 180 **degrees** form an opposition **aspect**. Since they are on opposing sides of the sky, planetary energies are polarized. Cooperation and awareness are necessary to foster growth; respect for diversity is required in order to get along. Planets in opposition may feel a combative or competitive drive, a need for compromise, a longing for separation, or a yearning for fulfillment. Planets in opposition share the same **sign mode** and **polarity**. According to the **Thema Mundi**, oppositions reflect the nature of **Saturn**. The strength of an opposition depends on the **orb** between the planets involved and is usually 8 degrees or less.

⟶ ✦ ⟵

orb, *noun*

An orb is a sphere of influence measured in **degrees** around a **planet**. Planets, **chart angles**, or other **chart** points in **aspect** to this orb experience the planet's effects. In medieval **astrology**, the radius of an orb was called the *moiety*; modern **astrologers** simply use the word *orb* for the radius. The number of degrees of allowable orb around a planet will vary by astrologer and by the planets involved, but it is usually 8–10 degrees or less.

⟶ ✦ ⟵

Pallas, *noun*

The **asteroid** Pallas—short for Pallas Athene, the Greek goddess of wisdom—represents themes such as wisdom, cunning, creative intelligence, strategy, skill, craft, and healing.

⟶ ✦ ⟵

part of fortune, *noun*

The part of fortune is a calculated point in an astrological **chart** representing manifestation or abundance, especially in the realm of money and possessions. It's often paired with the **part of spirit**. In **Hellenistic astrology**, the part of fortune is known as the "lot of the **Moon**."

············ ✦ ············

part of spirit, *noun*

The part of spirit is a calculated point in a **chart** that represents how you use your life circumstances to further your spiritual growth. It's often paired with the **part of fortune**. In **Hellenistic astrology**, the part of spirit is known as the "lot of the **Sun**."

············ ✦ ············

Pisces, *noun*

Pisces is best when allowed to drift, to float without judgment in everlasting bliss. Then, this **Jupiter**-ruled sign can commune with the cosmos. Pisceans strive to be in the world, yet not of it. The **constellation** associated with this **mutable water sign** is the Fish, two fish that are tied together. Pisceans may need to work to stay present, to reach for the stars without getting tangled up by their own feet.

Pisceans have romantic hearts, which can make for a beautiful relationship. But, on the other hand, they're just as likely to forget your anniversary as to woo you with their amorous gestures. Take comfort in the fact that it's not out of malice, just being lost in their own thoughts.

Modern astrology associates Pisces, as the twelfth **Zodiac sign**, with the **Twelfth House** via the **natural house** overlay. Some also say Pisces has a strong affinity with the planet **Neptune**.

Placidus houses, *noun*

Placidus houses are a time-divisional **quadrant house system** first developed by medieval Arab **astrologers**. The tools for calculation of the Placidus houses became the most widely published system in the late nineteenth century; hence, the system became the most popular of **modern astrology** in the twentieth century.

------------------- ✦ -------------------

planet, *noun*

Planet is a catchall term in **astrology** used to describe celestial objects that move. The word *planet* is derived from a Greek term meaning "wanderer" or "wandering star." As the active part of the heavens, the planets lie at the heart of the astrological model, forming the framework from which **Zodiac signs**, **houses**, and **aspects** derive their meanings.

The planets used in traditional **Western astrology** and **Indian astrology**—Mercury, Venus, Mars, Jupiter, and Saturn— are visible to the unaided eye. Modern **astrologers** have also incorporated the more recently discovered planets **Uranus** and **Neptune**, dwarf planets such as **Pluto** and **Ceres**, and numerous other **centaurs**, **asteroids**, and **trans-Neptunian objects** (TNOs). The **Sun** and **Moon** are often referred to as planets as well, for simplicity's sake.

In an astrology **chart**, the location of planets by Zodiac sign also determines their **essential dignity** and **house ruler**.

planet return, *noun*

When a planet returns to the same **degree** along the **Zodiac** at which it was located at birth, a person experiences a planet return. A planet return begins a new cycle for the planet involved; it's considered a useful technique for **astrological forecasting**. A **solar return** and a **Saturn return** are the most well-known planet return charts, but any planet can be used.

⋯⋯⋯⋯⋯ ✦ ⋯⋯⋯⋯⋯

planetary hours, *noun*

The planetary hours is a system for assigning each hour of the day to a governing **planet**. Days are divided into twelve equal parts from sunrise to sunset, and twelve more between sunset and sunrise; these parts are called hours. The ruling planets of each hour follow a repeating sequence known as the **Chaldean order**.

The Latin names for the seven days of the week are derived from the first planetary hour of that day. In English these became Sunday for the **Sun**, Monday for the **Moon**, Tuesday for **Mars**, Wednesday for **Mercury**, Thursday for **Jupiter**, Friday for **Venus**, and Saturday for **Saturn**.

Because astrological **charts** required significant mathematical knowledge and reference material to erect (remember, this was way before computers), oftentimes the planetary hours were used as a substitute, especially in **astrological magic**.

planetary joys, *noun*

The system of planetary joys defines a **planet**'s favorite **house**. Each of the seven visible planets has a planetary joy: **Mercury** joys in the **First House**, the **Moon** in the **Third House**, **Venus** in the **Fifth House**, **Mars** in the **Sixth House**, the **Sun** in the **Ninth House**, **Jupiter** in the **Eleventh House**, and **Saturn** in the **Twelfth House**. The planetary joys concept is a key ingredient in determining the original meanings of the houses.

.... ✦ ....

planetary sect, *noun*

In **traditional astrology**, **planets** are divided into two teams, known as sects. These teams are led by the **Sun** and the **Moon**. The planets **Jupiter** and **Saturn** are on the Sun's team; **Venus** and **Mars** are on the Moon's team. **Mercury** can join either sect.

When a birth time occurs in the daytime, the Sun's team is stronger in a **chart**; when a birth occurs at night, the Moon's team takes the stronger role.

Planetary sect plays a role in the meanings of **houses**, as well as the **essential dignity** determination of the **triplicity lords**.

Pluto, *noun*

Pluto's 248-year orbit is highly elliptical; he spends fourteen to thirty years in each **Zodiac sign**. Since Pluto was first spotted less than one hundred years ago, we've yet to experience Pluto in all the signs. Consequently, it's not clear what Pluto may signify. Some **astrologers** call him the most important **planet** in the sky. Others swear he has little impact.

Modern astrology associates Pluto with primordial creative and destructive forces. Where he sits may give insight into how we transform, transmute, regenerate, heal, renew, or purge. *Power* is another Pluto key word, in both the positive and negative sense. Pluto's also linked to the hidden, the occult, the taboo, or even the shameful.

Modern astrology first associated Pluto with the **Zodiac sign Aries**, then later with **Scorpio**. Via the **natural house** overlay, Pluto and Scorpio are linked to the **Eighth House**.

.... ✦ ....

polarity, *noun*

Zodiac signs are divided into two polarities: *diurnal signs*, called "day, masculine, or yang"; and *nocturnal signs*, called "night, feminine, or yin."

Planets in diurnal signs—**Aries**, **Gemini**, **Leo**, **Libra**, **Sagittarius**, and **Aquarius**—are sunny, outgoing, extroverted, and interested in what is going on in the external, objective, light-filled world. **Fire signs** and **air signs** are diurnal.

Planets in nocturnal signs—**Taurus**, **Cancer**, **Virgo**, **Scorpio**, **Capricorn**, and **Pisces**—are receptive, intuitive, introverted, or motivated by subjective reality. **Earth signs** and **water signs** are nocturnal.

precession (of the equinoxes), *noun*

The relationship between the Earth's **seasons** and the **ecliptic** is not fixed. Rather, the location of the **Sun** at the Spring **Equinox** moves clockwise (precesses) against the background of **fixed stars** at a rate of 1 **degree** every seventy-two years, for a full cycle of nearly twenty-six thousand years. Plato called this a Great Year; modern astronomers refer to the phenomenon as the precession of the equinoxes. The **Zodiac sign** in which the Spring Equinox is located is considered the current **astrological age.**

✦

Priapus, *noun*

As a counterpoint to the **Moon**'s apogee **Black Moon Lilith**, **astrologers** named the perigee point Priapus, signifying unrealized yet potent sexual energy. When the **New Moon** or **Full Moon** is **conjunct** Priapus, it's known as a **supermoon**. Priapus and Black Moon Lilith are the other names for the **lunar apsides.**

✦

progressions, *noun*

An **astrological forecasting** tool, progressions move the astrological **chart** forward or backward a symbolic amount of time to predict life events. The most commonly used form of progressions moves **planets** in a natal chart forward one day for each year of life; these are called secondary progressions.

psychological astrology, *noun*

Psychological astrology is a branch of **modern astrology** that developed in the mid-twentieth century through the combination of **astrology** with humanistic, depth, and transpersonal psychology. It incorporates ideas such as archetypes, synchronicities, subpersonalities, and psychological drives and needs so that the astrology **chart** becomes a tool for fostering psychological integration. Not all **astrologers** who practice psychological astrology are trained and licensed therapists, though some are.

.... ✦ ....

quadrant, *noun*

An **astrology chart** can be divided into four quadrants using the **chart angles.**

In **Hellenistic astrology**, quadrants included the **houses** on either side of the chart angles and related to the stages of life. The first quadrant (**Second, First**, and **Twelfth houses**) signifies youth; the second (**Eleventh, Tenth**, and **Ninth houses**), middle age; the third (**Eighth, Seventh**, and **Sixth houses**), old age; and the fourth (**Fifth, Fourth**, and **Third houses**), the soul after death.

In **modern astrology**, quadrants are often linked to psychological processes. **Planets** in the first quadrant (First, Second, and Third houses) signify the self and self-knowledge; the second (Fourth, Fifth, and Sixth houses), how the self relates to family and obligations; the third (Seventh, Eighth, and Ninth houses), how the self relates to partners and tribe; and the fourth (Tenth, Eleventh, and Twelfth houses), how the self relates to the world and the cosmic order.

House systems that use the chart angles as the **house cusps** for the start of the First, Fourth, Seventh, and Tenth houses are known as quadrant house systems.

Regulus, *noun*

Regulus marks the heart of the Lion in the **constellation Leo**. This **fixed star** lends a noble, generous, ambitious, or prideful tone to nearby **planets** or **chart angles**. Regulus is one the four **royal stars**, along with **Aldebaran, Antares,** and **Fomalhaut**. In **astrological magic**, Regulus is known as the Watcher of the North and is associated with the archangel Raphael. Due to **precession**, Regulus currently sits at 0 **degrees** of the **Tropical Zodiac** sign **Virgo**.

relationship astrology, *noun*

Relationship astrology uses techniques for comparing the **charts** of two or more people, events, or organizations to understand how one relates to the other, as well as suggest ways to create more harmonious and loving connections. Popular relationship astrology tools include synastry, composite, and Davison charts.

retrograde, *adjective*

A retrograde **planet** appears to move along the **ecliptic** contrary to its usual forward, or direct, motion. Since retrogrades occur when another planet is closest to Earth in its orbit, retrograde planets beyond the Earth's orbit appear brighter in the night sky than at other times. Retrograde planets are said to express themselves more subjectively or intensely than direct planets. All planets turn retrograde; the **Sun** and **Moon** do not. When a planet begins or ends its retrograde it's called a station.

rising sign, *noun*

The **Zodiac sign** in which the **ascendant** of a **chart** is located, the rising sign indicates physical form, personal style, and lifestyle. In **modern astrology**, the three factors that, taken together, best summarize overall personality and character are the rising sign, **Sun sign**, and **Moon sign**.

✦

royal stars, *noun*

The royal stars are four bright **fixed stars** along the **ecliptic**— **Aldebaran**, **Regulus**, **Antares**, and **Fomalhaut**. Alignments with these stars may herald significant world events.

✦

rulership, *noun*

Rulership is an **essential dignity** based on the **seasons**. The bright, swiftly moving lights of the **Moon** and **Sun** rule over the signs **Cancer** and **Leo**. These two **Zodiac signs** govern the warmest part of the year after the Northern **Hemisphere**'s Summer **Solstice**. The slowest and dimmest **planet** visible to the naked eye, **Saturn**, rules over the signs **Capricorn** and **Aquarius**. These two signs govern the coldest part of the year after the Winter Solstice.

The remaining visible planets also rule two signs each, arranged based on their apparent speed—**Mercury**, closest to the Sun, rules the two signs **Virgo** and **Gemini**. Next is **Venus** ruling **Libra** and **Taurus**, **Mars** ruling **Scorpio** and **Aries**, and **Jupiter** ruling **Sagittarius** and **Pisces**. Each planet rules one sign of each **polarity**, representing their dual natures, except the Sun and Moon, which serve as complementary polarities to each other.

.... ✦ ....

Sagittarius, *noun*

Sagittarius's desire to know—to learn, to expand, to see the world—is its deepest motivating force. Thanks to its **Jupiter**-ruled nature, the Sagittarius sign believes in essential cosmic goodness. As a **fire sign**, its enthusiasm and zeal can be infectious.

However, in their quest for their grand vision, Sagittarians can miss the important details. Sagittarians are happy to have your company on their adventure, but it's the adventure, not you, that's paramount. Given their **mutable** tendency, they aren't known for their long attention spans, unless they are fascinated by the subject. To keep them hooked, make sure they are never bored.

Sagittarius's **constellation** is the Archer, traditionally a centaur drawing a bow. The half-human, half-beast nature suggests the Sagittarius sign strives to use the mind to tame the instinctual.

Modern astrology associates Sagittarius, as the ninth **Zodiac sign**, with the **Ninth House** via the **natural house** overlay.

Saturn, *noun*

Ringed Saturn is the slowest of the visible **planets**, taking nearly thirty years to make one full circuit of the **ecliptic**, and spending around two-and-a-half years in each **Zodiac sign**.

Saturn is associated with age, sobriety, and limits. Wherever he is, we feel more committed, mature, and responsible.

Saturn encourages focus on the here and now. It's through his slow and steady approach that he builds structures meant to endure lifetimes.

Saturn's known as the greater **malefic**. Too much saturnine energy results in some of the most negative human feelings: depression, betrayal, isolation, fear, and rigidity.

Saturn rules the **Zodiac signs Aquarius** and **Capricorn**. His **planetary joy** is the **Twelfth House**. Saturday is Saturn's day of the week. In **astrological magic**, Saturn's colors are black, dark blue, and browns. His alchemical metal is lead. The adjective associated with Saturn is *saturnine*.

Via the **natural house** overlay, **modern astrology** associates Saturn with the **Tenth House**.

✦

Saturn return, *noun*

A Saturn return is a **planet return** that occurs once every twenty-nine to thirty years, when Saturn returns to the same **degree** along the **Zodiac** at which it was located at the moment of birth. Saturn returns bring up questions about what it means to be an adult, how you're meeting your responsibilities, or what you want to be "when you grow up." It's one of the astrological events that lead some to seek out astrological advice for the first time.

Scorpio, *noun*

Scorpios may be secretive and controlling, but there's a good reason. As a **fixed water sign**, Scorpio feels so deeply that it's not easy to bring things to the surface. Scorpios feel so intensely, secrecy and control are sensible solutions to feel safe. **Mars**-ruled Scorpios develop tremendous inner strength and courage just to survive in their own skin.

Trust doesn't come easy, but once a Scorpio commits, they are loyal till the end. When they feel safe enough to talk, consider it an honor and listen without judgment.

The Scorpio **constellation** is the Scorpion; it's also associated in mythology with the eagle or the phoenix.

Modern astrology associates Scorpio, as the eighth **Zodiac sign**, with the **Eighth House** via the **natural house** overlay. Since the 1960s, **astrologers** have also given it an affinity with **Pluto**.

······· ✦ ·······

seasons, *noun*

Thanks to the Earth's 23½-**degree** tilt, our **planet** experiences four seasons: spring, summer, fall, and winter. **Equinoxes** mark the beginning of spring and fall; **solstices** mark the beginning of summer and winter. The **Tropical Zodiac** aligns with these four seasons, forming the **world axis**.

Second House, *noun*

When the **Sun** is in the Second House, it "emerges" from the underworld into the predawn sky, which is why the original name for this **house** was the Gate of Hades. For the ancient **astrologers**, riches also came out of the ground—precious metals and stones, as well as crops that sustain life. So it's a house that's associated with wealth, assets, and other resources.

As the Second House is a **succedent house**, it contains what supports the **First House**; that's all the things we store up to help us navigate the world, sometimes called our movable possessions.

The Second House sits opposite the **Eighth House**.

Via the **natural house** overlay, **modern astrology** associates the Second House with **Taurus**, **Venus**, or both. Its modern key words include *values* and *self-worth*.

✦

Seventh House, *noun*

The Seventh House sits opposite the **First House**, so it plays host to what's *not* you, that is to say, the "other" in your life. The Seventh House contains important others—your spouse, your partners (business and romantic)—as well as the other side of a debate, the other team, or even your adversaries or competitors.

The **descendant** is associated with the Seventh House, which makes it one of the **angular houses**.

Via the **natural house** overlay, **modern astrology** associates the Seventh House with **Libra**, **Venus**, or both.

sextile, *noun*

Planets that form a sextile **aspect** are 60 **degrees** apart from one another along the **ecliptic**. Planetary energies flow smoothly with a little effort, so they suggest openness into new possibilities and connections. Sextiles between planets feel cooperative, friendly, harmonious, pleasant, easy, relaxed, helpful, and lazy. Planets in sextile sit in **Zodiac signs** that share the same **polarity**. According to the **Thema Mundi**, sextiles reflect the nature of **Venus**. The strength of a sextile depends on the **orb** between the planets involved and is usually 4–6 degrees or less.

⋯⋯⋯ ✦ ⋯⋯⋯

Sidereal Zodiac, *noun*

The Sidereal Zodiac is based on the position of the **fixed stars**—not the **seasons** as the **Tropical Zodiac** is. To preserve the appearance of the correct **constellation** behind the **planets**, the Sidereal Zodiac takes the **precession** into account and moves the starting point of the Zodiac 1 **degree** every seventy-two years. As of 2019, the Sidereal Zodiac's starting point is equivalent to 24 degrees **Aries** on the Tropical Zodiac. The Sidereal Zodiac is most often used by those practicing **Indian astrology**.

This difference between the Sidereal and Tropical Zodiacs leads to confusion among those new to **astrology**, since it means people have a different **Zodiac sign** in each tradition. For example, if you have a **Gemini Sun sign** using a Tropical Zodiac, you may have a **Taurus** Sun sign using the Sidereal Zodiac. **Astrologers** continue to research and debate the subject.

sign mode, *noun*

There are three **Zodiac** sign modes—**cardinal signs, fixed signs,** and **mutable signs.** Sign modes indicate whether a sign falls at the beginning, middle, or end of a season, suggesting subtle qualities about **Zodiac signs** based on shifting **seasons.** Modes are also known as quadruplicities.

⋯⋯⋯⋯ ✦ ⋯⋯⋯⋯

Sixth House, *noun*

The Sixth House is the **planetary joy** of **Mars.** It's really just a **house** of stuff that takes effort to accomplish. So, the Sixth House is a place of hard work, of those who work hard, or those who work for you. It is also a house of all the duties and obligations that require effort to fulfill.

It contains health and illness; maintaining your own body is a kind of obligation so that it can serve you in return. It's also the house of small, domesticated animals and pets—from the days when domesticated animals also had a job to do.

The Sixth House is one of the **cadent houses**; it sits opposite the **Twelfth House,** the planetary joy of **Saturn.**

Via the **natural house** overlay, **modern astrology** associates the Sixth House with **Virgo, Mercury,** or both.

solar arc, *noun*

A solar arc is an **astrological forecasting** tool that uses symbolic time to predict life events. A variant of **progressions**, a solar arc **chart** moves all **planets** forward at the same rate as the **Sun** moves.

✦

solar return, *noun*

A solar return is a **planet return** that occurs each year when the **Sun** returns to the same **degree** along the **ecliptic** it occupied at your moment of birth. This is considered your astrological birthday. A solar return **chart** is a tool used in **astrological forecasting** to predict events and decisions to be made in the upcoming year.

✦

solstice, *noun*

A term derived from two Latin words meaning "Sun standstill," solstices mark the start of the summer and winter **seasons**. At the Summer Solstice, the day is the longest of the year; at the Winter Solstice, the night is the longest. In the **Tropical Zodiac**, solstices occur when the **Sun** enters **Cancer** and **Capricorn**. These signs form part of the **world axis**. In the Northern **Hemisphere**, the Summer Solstice falls at 0 **degrees** Cancer and the Winter Solstice falls at 0 degrees Capricorn; in the Southern Hemisphere, this is reversed.

south node (of the Moon), *noun*

The south **lunar node**, also called the descending node, Dragon's Tail, or Ketu, represents easy talents, dissolution, and the act of letting go. In karmic and **evolutionary astrology**, the south node's **Zodiac sign** and **house** location indicate the direction from which the soul is growing away, having already learned lessons in this area.

✦

square, *noun*

Planets making a square **aspect** to one another are separated by 90 **degrees** along the **ecliptic**. Squares connote achievement through strife. Though the planetary energies conflict, through effort over time the internal and creative tensions can bring rich rewards. Common astrological key words for squares include *challenge, clashes, crisis, discord, frustration, friction, stress, struggle, irritation*, and *cross-purpose*.

Planets square one another sit in **Zodiac signs** with the same **sign mode** but a different **polarity** and **element**. In other words, they have the same style in taking action in the world, but they often have conflicting goals or motivations. Hence the friction. According to the **Thema Mundi**, squares reflect the nature of **Mars**.

The strength of a square depends on the **orb** between the planets involved and is usually 6–8 degrees or less.

succedent houses, *noun*

Succedent houses contain things that assist the neighboring **angular house**. **Planets** in these houses are of average strength, and serve in a supporting role in a **chart**. The succedent houses are the **Second**, **Fifth**, **Eighth**, and **Eleventh houses.**

$$+$$

Sun, *noun*

The Sun symbolizes life, vitality, and energy, and the related fields of healing and purifying. By its light, we see and comprehend the natural world. It's associated with our awareness and the power to make conscious choices. It also governs things that require clear sight, such as witnessing and prophesying.

As the center of our solar system, the Sun represents leaders, as well as the benefits, honors, and rewards of leadership. To the ancients, the Sun was the cosmic lawgiver.

Conversely, an unskillful expression of the Sun includes pride, arrogance, or a lack of enthusiasm for life.

The Sun rules the **Zodiac sign Leo**. His **planetary joy** is the **Ninth House**. Sunday is the Sun's day of the week. In **astrological magic**, Sun colors are warm, ranging from yellow to orange, red, and gold. His alchemical metal is gold.

Via the **natural house** overlay, **modern astrology** associates the Sun with the **Fifth House**.

Sun sign, *noun*

The **Zodiac** sign in which the **Sun** is located, your Sun sign indicates the ways you shine, your vitality, your conscious choices, and your leadership style. In **modern astrology**, the three factors that, taken together, best summarize overall personality and character are the Sun sign, **Moon sign**, and **rising sign**. Popular **horoscopes** are written using Sun sign **astrology**.

.... ✦ ....

supermoon, *noun*

A supermoon is a **Full Moon** or **New Moon** that occurs when the **Moon** is near its perigee, the point in its orbit when it's closest to the Earth. A Full Moon supermoon will appear 15 percent larger and about 30 percent brighter than an average Full Moon. It's said to signify times of intense emotions and passions.

.... ✦ ....

Taurus, *noun*

Slowing down and indulging in all the world's sensual pleasures is a Taurean passion. Taurus has a natural gift for staying grounded and centered, weathering storms that would blow other **Zodiac signs** away. (Of course, this **Venus**-ruled **earth sign** would prefer to be properly outfitted for the weather first.)

Taureans respect peace, loyalty, patience, and promise-keeping. But keep waving that red cape in front of them and you'll certainly face the pointy end of their horns (the Bull is the symbol of Taurus, after all). Nothing annoys a Taurus more than constant change, especially if you expect them to do the changing. Given their **fixed sign** nature, take care when moving them before they are ready—at best, they'll stage a sit-in; at worst, you'll find the raging Bull charging at you.

Modern astrology associates Taurus, as the second **Zodiac** sign, with the **Second House** via the **natural house** overlay.

⋯⋯⋯ ✦ ⋯⋯⋯

Tenth House, *noun*

The Tenth House sits at the top of the **chart**. When the **Sun** is in the Tenth House, it's at its high point in the middle of the day; consequently, the Tenth House is associated with what elevates you. That includes your highest potential, your "calling" or vocation, your reputation, and your purpose in the world. In modern times, we associate it with your career or profession. The Tenth House also represents authority— where you have authority or those who have authority over you, such as bosses, landlords, or government officials.

The Tenth House is one of the **angular houses**. The **midheaven** marks the cusp of the Tenth House in **quadrant house systems**. It sits opposite the **Fourth House**.

Via the **natural house** overlay, **modern astrology** associates the Tenth House with **Capricorn**, **Saturn**, or both.

Thema Mundi, *noun*

The earliest teaching **chart** in **Hellenistic astrology**, the Thema Mundi represents the chart of the creation of the world, or the world soul. **Houses**, **aspects**, the **world axis**, and other astrological concepts derive from the Thema Mundi.

⋯⋯⋯ ✦ ⋯⋯⋯

Third House, *noun*

The Third House contains everything familiar to you. This includes your siblings, your neighbors, or the coworkers you see every day. It also describes your habits, routines, and the places you visit on a regular basis—short trips to school or work or the grocery store. In other words, it's your comfort zone.

Via the **natural house** overlay, **modern astrology** associates the Third House with **Gemini** and **Mercury**. But its original name was the House of the Moon, or Moon Goddess. Ancient deities related to both Mercury and the **Moon** were responsible for delivering messages, writing, communications, record keeping, and paperwork; so these, too, fall under the domain of the Third House.

The Third House is one of the **cadent houses**; its opposite is the **Ninth House**, the House of the **Sun**.

traditional astrology, *noun*

Traditional astrology, sometimes called classical astrology, includes astrology practiced in the West before the age of the Scientific Revolution.

After the decline of the Hellenistic and Roman empires, Islamic culture kept the **Western astrology** flame alive. Arab astrology devised new **house systems**, additional parts beyond the **part of fortune, part of spirit**, and other Hellenistic lots, as well as its own lunar astrology.

As **Hellenistic astrology** flowed into the Christian West, the religious or spiritual aspects of astrology were de-emphasized. Nevertheless, astrology remained a core symbolic language of the Western esoteric tradition, influencing works of art and culture such as Dante's *Divine Comedy*, Shakespeare's plays, and the art of Botticelli. Medieval and Renaissance astrology focused on **astrological forecasting, horary astrology, mundane astrology, medical astrology, electional astrology**, and **astrological magic**.

+

transit, *noun*

While a birth **chart** is a snapshot of the position of **planets** at a particular place and time, the sky is always moving. A transit occurs when a planet moves to the same zodiacal **degree** a planet occupied in your birth chart, or when a planet moves to form an **aspect** to this degree. Transits signify an intensification or energy involving these planets and are one of **modern astrology**'s most popular **astrological forecasting** techniques.

When the transiting planet meets itself by **conjunction**, the transit is called a **planet return**.

trans-Neptunian objects, *noun*

Astronomers continue to discover dwarf **planets** like **Pluto** and other minor planets beyond the orbit of **Neptune**, collectively called trans-Neptunian objects (TNOs). Some **astrologers** add these minor planets to their **charts**, interpreting their meanings based primarily on the significance of their mythological names. Trans-Neptunian objects now being used in **astrology** include Eris, Haumea, Makemake, and Sedna; astronomers may discover hundreds more.

·················· + ··················

trine, *noun*

Planets form a trine **aspect** when they are separated by 120 **degrees** along the **ecliptic**. Trines suggest these planets share an expansive, happy feeling of being supported by the cosmos itself, as well as one another. Trines between planets suggest their relationship is beneficial, enthusiastic, rewarding, joyful, lucky, optimistic, merciful, overindulgent, or lazy.

Planets that trine one another sit in **Zodiac signs** that share the same **polarity** and **element**, and therefore experience a close affinity. According to the **Thema Mundi**, trines reflect the nature of **Jupiter**.

The strength of a trine depends on the **orb** between the planets involved and is usually around 6–8 degrees or less.

triplicity, *noun*

In **Hellenistic astrology**, triplicities are four groups of signs formed by affinity with the **solstices** and **equinoxes**. Each triplicity includes one **cardinal sign** and the two signs that **trine** it. As **astrology** developed, the four classical Greek **elements**—fire, earth, air, and water—were assigned to the triplicities, creating what we now call **fire signs**, **earth signs**, **air signs**, and **water signs**.

Triplicity provides another type of **essential dignity**. Triplicity lords—planets that govern triplicities—are assigned by **planetary sect**.

$$\cdots\cdots\cdots\; + \;\cdots\cdots\cdots$$

Tropical Zodiac, *noun*

In the Tropical Zodiac, the twelve **Zodiac signs** are determined by their relationship to the seasonal turning points: the **solstices** and **equinoxes**. The word *tropical* comes from ancient Greek words meaning "to turn" or a "turning point."

Due to the phenomenon of **precession**, the Tropical Zodiac no longer aligns with the **Astronomical Zodiac** constellations. Since the Spring Equinox marked the new year at the time **Hellenistic astrology** developed, the Tropical Zodiac begins with **Aries**, the **constellation** in which the **Sun** was located at that time.

Those who practice **Western astrology** typically use the Tropical Zodiac.

Twelfth House, *noun*

Known as the **planetary joy** of **Saturn**, the Twelfth House's original name was the House of Bad Spirit. It's the little critical negative voice that plagues us with fear and doubts.

Saturn sets limits and boundaries, but it can also signify going on retreat or sabbatical. Isolation and separation is a necessary part of life, but it's certainly not an easy part. This would certainly be a **house** that could be called the Dark Night of the Soul, where we must confront the hidden, unseen, and unconscious side of our natures. It's in solitude and silence where we also reach life's mystical experiences; these, too, are contained in the Twelfth House.

Via the **natural house** overlay, **modern astrology** associates the Twelfth House with **Pisces**, **Jupiter**, **Neptune**, or all of them. Modern key words associated with it also include *spirituality* and *sensitivity*.

It is one of the **cadent houses.**

✦

Uranus, *noun*

Uranus sits on the border between the visible and invisible. In 1781, with the aid of a telescope, Sir William Herschel discovered this: the first **planet** beyond the visible planets. That moment began the era of **modern astrology.**

Modern **astrologers** associate Uranus with liberation of all forms. He's the impulse to individuate, to shed our skin so we may become more. Uranus incites revolution to overthrow the status quo. Where he is, we seek to awaken, to shock, or to rebel.

At his best, Uranus brings genius, innovation, iconoclasm, and eccentricity. At his worst and least skilled, Uranian energies become extremist, reactive, erratic, chaotic, wantonly destructive, and traumatizing.

Modern astrology associates Uranus with the **Zodiac sign Aquarius**. Via the **natural house** overlay, Uranus and Aquarius are linked to the **Eleventh House**.

⋯⋯⋯ ✦ ⋯⋯⋯

Venus, *noun*

The sparkling jewel of the heavens, Venus is the brightest object in the sky after the **Sun** and **Moon**. Pleasure in all its forms celebrates Venus. She governs desire, beauty, and things that soothe and delight our senses, entertain us, and bring us satisfaction. Venus seeks to relate, socialize, reconcile, harmonize, unite, and love.

Called the lesser **benefic**, Venus's pleasures tend to fade quickly. At her most demanding, Venus seeks to acquire, possess, purchase, or own. The dark side of Venus includes vanity, lust, jealousy, envy, self-indulgence, and obsession.

Venus rules the **Zodiac signs Libra** and **Taurus**. Her **planetary joy** is the **Fifth House**. Friday is Venus's day of the week. In **astrological magic**, colors associated with Venus include white, pink, pastels, and green. Her alchemical metal is copper. The adjectives associated with Venus are *venial* and *venereal*.

Via the **natural house** overlay, **modern astrology** associates Venus with the **Second** and **Seventh houses**.

Vesta, *noun*

The **asteroid** Vesta, Roman goddess of the hearth and virginity, represents themes of self-sufficiency, sexual nonattachment, purity, and fulfillment of obligations.

.... ✛ ....

Virgo, *noun*

Virgos are more than capable of taking care of themselves and others. The Virgo **constellation** depicts a woman carrying a sheaf of wheat. *Virgo* means "virgin," or "a woman whole unto herself"; she brings what's needed to survive in the material world.

On the flip side, Virgos desperately seek perfection. While calm and competent on the outside, they often struggle with self-criticism. For this **Mercury**-ruled **earth sign**, the best approach is to focus on step-by-step improvements. The **mutable** nature of Virgos allows them to analyze the situation, adapt, and move forward, if they can forgive their own imperfections.

Friends, family, and partners of Virgos can show their unconditional respect and open appreciation by listening nonjudgmentally to their concerns.

Modern astrology associates Virgo, as the sixth **Zodiac sign**, with the **Sixth House** via the **natural house** overlay. Other **astrologers** have asserted that the **centaur Chiron**, the dwarf planet **Ceres**, and the **asteroid Vesta** have an affinity with Virgo.

void-of-course Moon, *noun*

A void-of-course Moon occurs once the **Moon** has made the last major **aspect** to a visible **planet**, but before it has entered the next **Zodiac sign**. Void Moons lack the *oomph* to launch new projects, but are perfect for recharging, catching up, or doing deep work. **Astrologers** practicing **electional astrology** or **astrological magic** seek to circumvent void Moons when planning auspicious occasions.

———— ✦ ————

water sign, *noun*

Zodiacal signs are each associated with one of the four Greek **elements**: air, fire, water, and earth; the Greeks believed these four elements made up the physical universe. The water element encourages strong feelings and expressing yourself in instinctual, emotional ways. **Cancer**, **Scorpio**, and **Pisces** are water signs.

———— ✦ ————

Western astrology, *noun*

Western astrology is a catchall phrase for the astrological descendants of **Hellenistic astrology**, including **traditional astrology** and **modern astrology**. Western **astrologers** typically use the **Tropical Zodiac**, which is often used in popular **Sun sign horoscopes**.

whole sign houses, *noun*

One of the idealized **house systems**, whole sign **houses** simply use **Zodiac sign** boundaries as **house cusps**. The sign in which the **ascendent** sits becomes the **First House**; the **midheaven** may fall anywhere between the **Seventh** and **Twelfth houses**. Whole sign houses are the earliest house system, used in **Hellenistic astrology** all the way through the early Middle Ages. The whole sign system appears primarily in **traditional astrology** and in **Indian astrology**, in which it's considered the primary or seed **chart**. It's also used in writing **Sun sign horoscopes**.

✛

world axis, *noun*

In **mundane astrology**, the world axis represents collective human affairs. The world axis is defined as the location of the **Sun** at the **solstices** and **equinoxes**, or 0 **degrees** of the **cardinal signs Aries, Cancer, Libra**, and **Capricorn**. **Planets conjunct**, or otherwise in **aspect** to these degrees in a **chart**, may suggest a strong link to social or global events.

✛

Zodiac, *noun*

The Zodiac is the band of **ecliptic**-crossing **constellations**. The word *Zodiac* derives from a Greek word loosely translated as "the way of life."

Dividing this band in different ways produces **astrology**'s three major Zodiacs—the **Tropical Zodiac**, the **Sidereal Zodiac**, and the **Astronomical Zodiac**. Those who practice **Western astrology** typically use the Tropical Zodiac. This contrasts with **Indian astrology**, which adopted a star-based Sidereal Zodiac that more closely aligned with the constellations, and with astronomers, who refer to the thirteen officially designated constellations of the Astronomical Zodiac.

But having three Zodiacs often means that the same person could wind up with three different **Sun signs**. This confusion leads to news stories claiming **Zodiac signs** are changing, or that **horoscopes** use the wrong signs.

⋯⋯⋯⋯ ✦ ⋯⋯⋯⋯

Zodiac sign, *noun*

Zodiac signs are mathematically equal divisions of a **Zodiac**, used for describing a location along the **ecliptic**.

The familiar **Sun sign** Zodiac features twelve 30-**degree** divisions of the ecliptic, approximating the **Sun**'s movement through the year's twelve months. Though these solar Zodiac signs—**Aries**, **Taurus**, **Gemini**, **Cancer**, **Leo**, **Virgo**, **Libra**, **Scorpio**, **Sagittarius**, **Capricorn**, **Aquarius**, and **Pisces**—are named after the ecliptic-crossing **constellations** of the **Astronomical Zodiac**, they are not the same thing.

Zodiacs that describe the **Moon**'s movement over a month's twenty-seven-and-a-third days are together known as **Lunar Zodiac** signs.

Acknowledgments

Books are a team effort. So is astrology.

First thanks must go to the myriad generations of astrologers whose enduring hunger for the heavens has kept astrology alive through the centuries. That this book exists in the twenty-first century is a testament to astrology's ability to enflame the imagination and inspire the soul.

In the digital age, our "cosmic science" is experiencing a new renaissance. All astrology lovers owe a debt to the generation of astrologers making astrology widely available through computer programs, Internet resources, online communities, and mobile apps. My special thanks go to Enid Newberg and the Kepler College team for their tireless efforts over the past two decades raising the bar for astrological education.

The definitions in this dictionary are excerpted from my astrology chart-reading courses hosted by AstrologyHub .com. Brava and many thanks to *Astrology Hub* founder Amanda Walsh and her A-Team angels for creating such a welcoming community for thousands of new astrology lovers and spiritual seekers to share their passion.

I'd like to extend my thanks to the folks at Adams Media who helped make this book possible. A special shout-out to Julia Jacques, who's been a great editor and huge help through the whole process.

I don't think I'd finish anything these days without Robin Langford, my friend, business coach, astrology student, and no-nonsense cheerleader. I may not like being asked, "So, are you done yet?" but it makes the magic happen.

Finally, I'd like to thank my mom, who bought me my first dictionary and read it to me, and my dad, who took me out to watch the stars. This book may not have been what they had in mind, but it wouldn't have been possible without them.

About the Author

Though Donna Woodwell attended grad school to become a foreign correspondent, she had no idea how foreign she'd get. After exploring ancient and modern astrological, magical, and mystical practices for more than twenty-five years, today she uses this wisdom to help folks discover—and live—their unique genius. Since teaching at major astrology conferences, Kepler College, and *Astrology Hub*, Donna now runs her own school combining astrology and magic with self-mastery. Learn more at DonnaPhilosophica.com.